Investing for Couch Potatoes
Concise Edition

Tony Pow

Why you want to read this book

It should improve your financial health substantially.

- This book has more than 65 pages (6*9) and is about double the size of its competitors with similar price range.

- A best seller was written by a young writer whose main income was from his books and none from his investing. Most of my income is from investing.

- Many popular books claiming the authors making millions. However, usually their techniques are hard to follow. Many admitted they had been bankrupted many times. My techniques minimize risking our money. Paper test your technique first. I prefer to be a 'turtle investor'.

- There are many popular books combining technical and some fundamentals. They worked very well at one time and folks making millions following the advices. However, look at their recent performances of the last five years.

- One book describes ROE as the only theme (with the story of the life of the author to fill up the book). This book includes many basic metrics such as P/E.

My motivation to write this book

I would like to share my experiences, both good and bad. I use simple-to-follow techniques using the free (or low-cost) resources available to us.

My article

It could be the top-performed article in Seeking Alpha, an investing site, for recommending 10 or more stocks in a year from its published date. So far, no one challenges me. I will not write another similar article as I cannot top this one. However, the reasons why I selected these stocks are included in my books.

https://seekingalpha.com/article/2492255-a-tale-of-2-portfolios

Contents

Why you want to read this book 2

    Highlight: The power of market timing 4

Introduction 8

I Market timing on market crashes 13

    1   Simplest market timing 14

II Market correction 16

    2   Do 16

III Market timing by calendar 18

    3   Do 18

IV Finding Stocks 20

    4 Finviz's screener 20

V   Research stock by fundamentals 22

    5   Do 22

        Fundamental metrics 24

        Finviz parameters 35

        Summary 38

VI   Research stocks by Technical Analysis 40

    6   Do 40

VII   Bonus 42

    7   The best strategy 42

    8   Tom's conservative strategy 44

    9   Trade plan 46

    10   A turnaround strategy for value stocks 50

Appendix 1 – All my books 53

Appendix 2 – Complete Art of Investing 55

Appendix 3 - Our window to the investing world 58

Appendix 4 - ETFs / Mutual Funds 59

    Quick analysis of ETFs 66

    Rotation of 4 ETFs 68

Epilogue 69

Highlight: The power of market timing

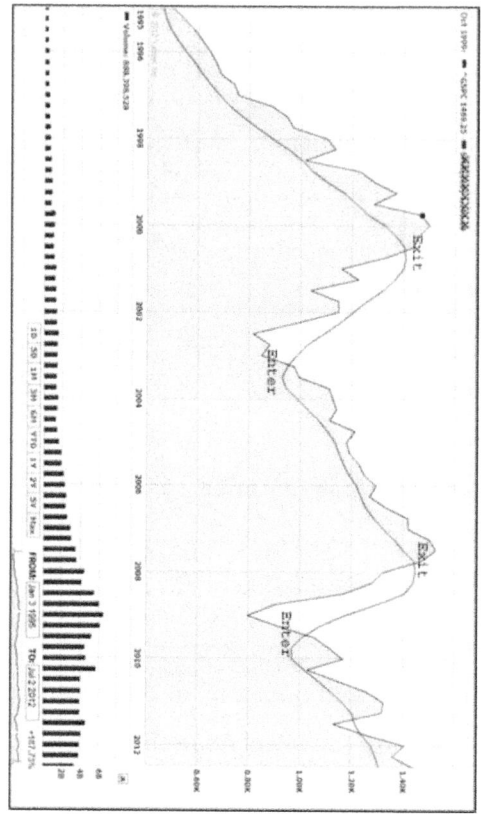

Most e-book readers allow you to select the graph to make it fit entirely to your screen. Detecting market plunges indicates the exit points and reentry points from 2000 to 9-2009 as follows.

Table: Vital Dates

Market Plunge	Peak	Bottom	Indicator Exit	Indicator Reenter
2000	08/28/00	09/20/02	10/01/00	06/01/03
2007	10/12/07	03/06/09	02/01/08	09/01/09
			08/01/11	11/01/11

As of 04/2014, my chart (from Yahoo!Finance) still indicates to invest fully in the market. For simplicity I skip a few brief exits and reentries since 2011. Run the simple chart once a month. When it indicates a potential market plunge is closer, run the chart once a week.

It is based on stock prices so it may not identify the peaks and bottoms precisely, but so far it has never failed to avoid big losses and ensure big gains by reentering the market. Hope it will give us enough time to act in the next market plunge as the last two did.

Unbelievable return with market timing

Calculate how much you made if you followed the above exit points and reenter points from 2000 to today. I bet you would make a good fortune.

To test the effect of market timing, I calculated the return of S&P 500 with market timing and compare it to the return of S&P 500 without market timing from 1-2000 to 9-2013.

There are many assumptions to make the calculations easier. In general, dividends are not considered. Compounding is not considered in most cases. The return with market timing should be substantially better if we buy a contra ETF during exits and sell it during reentries.

I was shocked by the incredible return by using simple market timing and the chart tells us to exit and reenter the market only 3 times from 2000 to 2013.
Summary info:

S&P 500 1-2000 to 9-2013	With Market Timing	Without Market Timing
Better	**500%**	
Gain	1,000	167
Gain %	68%	11%
Annualized gained	5%	1%
Days	4,959	4,959

Calculations:

S & P 500	With Market Timing	Without Market Timing
1-2000	1,469[1]	1,469[1]
Exit 10/01/00	1,041[2]	1,041
Enter 06/01/03	1,041	964[4]
Exit 02/01/08	1,489[3]	1,379[4]
Enter 09/01/09	1489	1,020[5]
Exit 08/01/11	1,888	1,293

Enter 11/01/11	1,888	1,251
09/03/13	2,469	1.638
Gained	2,469 – 1,469=1,000	1,638-1,469=167
Gain %	1000/1469 = 68%	167/1469 = 11%
Annualized gained	68% * 365/4959=5%	11%*365/4959=1%
Better	(1,000-167)/167 = 500%	

Portfolio with Market Timing:

[1] Both start with S&P 500 of 1,469 on 1-3-2000.

[2] 10/01/00
The market timing portfolio exits the market and remains same value of 1,041 until 6/1/00.

[3] 02/01/08
The market timing portfolio exits the market and remains same value of 1,489 until 9/1/09.

'1,489' is calculated as follows:
1,041 * (1 + Rate) = 1,041 * (1 + 1,379-964)/964) = 1,489
where S&P 500 is 964 on 6/1/00 and 1,379 on 2/1/08.

The other calculations are based on S&P 500 is 1,020 on 9/1/9, 1,293 on 8/1/11, 1,251 on 11/1/11 and 1,636 on 9/3/13.

Portfolio without Market Timing:

[1] Both starts with S&P 500 of 1,469 on 1-3-2000. We could use the 9/3/13 S&P 500 value, but it will not account on some compounded interest consideration.

[4] S&P 500 is 964 in 6/1/00 and 1,379 on 2/1/08.

[5] 02/01/08. The portfolio value is calculated to be 1,020 as follows:
1,379 * (1 + Rate) = 1,379 * (1 + (1020-1379)/1379) = 1,020
where S&P 500 is 1,379 on 2/1/08 and 1,020 on 9/1/09.

The other calculations are based on S&P 500 is 1,293 on 8/1/11, 1,251 on 11/1/11 and 1,636 on 9/3/13.

I cannot believe the shocking return with market timing. I checked my calculation and there was nothing wrong but do not hold me on this. Ignoring the compound rate of return should be minor. If you have time, send me your e-mail address to pow_tony@yahoo.com, so I can send you the spreadsheet to check out any error.

Even if I made a mistake somehow and got 100% instead of 500%, it still doubles the return without market timing! Ask any fund manager what it means to his or her fund performance and his / her career.

It will detect the next market plunges, but it may not give us ample of time to react as the last two did. It will not detect the precise bottoms and peaks as they depend on the stock price of an ETF representing the market. I have separate statistics on market peaks and bottoms but they have not been proven. The above may not work as effectively if there are too many followers. On the contrary it may work as it could be a self-fulfilling prophesy. The stock prices of SPY are obtained from Yahoo!Finance. The entry and exit points are obtained from my simple chart from Yahoo!Finance described and they are subject to my interpretation

The above uses charts using Single Moving Average for the last 350 days.

It can be created by following the steps; you need to create one yourself to detect the next plunge with current data.
- From Yahoo!Finance or any chart systems, enter SPY (or S&P 500 index) or an ETF that represents the total market.
- Select Interactive Chart.
- Click Technical Indicators.
- Select SMA (simple moving average).
- Enter 350 days (actually it is trade sessions). Many chart systems use 'month' as unit, enter 12 or 11.67 if decimals is allowed (=350/12) instead of 350.
- Enter 1-3-2000 on "FROM:" or any "from date" that fits your screen.
- Select Draw.

Note. I switch to Fidelity for charting now as I cannot produce the same info from Yahoo!Finance. It could be my fault or a bug that should be fixed. If you cannot use Fidelity, use StockCharts.com.

Introduction

This book is targeted to beginner investors and/or couch potatoes who do not want to spend a lot of time in managing their investments.

This book helps someone looking for simple but profitable strategies in investing. It only takes about half an hour a month to monitor the market and decide what stocks to buy and sell.

This book uses the advanced strategies described in my other books but in very simplified instructions. The trick is to make them easy to use from the research information available to us free of charge.

In general, the first chapter in each section tells you what to do (the 'Do' chapter) in very simple terms. The other chapters in each section explain the detail and you can skip them for now.

I start with market timing. You should not buy any stocks when the market is plunging. Actually you should sell most of the stocks you own when the market is plunging. For those who can take more risk, buy contra ETFs betting the market is plunging. I have a simple way to spot market plunges. It is based on charts. However, you can obtain similar info without creating charts and there is nothing to subscribe and buy. Although past performances are not guarantee for the future, following the techniques that work for the last two crashes (as of 6/2017) is better than not using any technique.

The chart tells us when to reenter the market for the best opportunity to make money. I did in 2003 and 2009.

Corrections provide opportunities to buy stocks. However, you have to prepare for the next correction by accumulating cash in advance and preparing a list of stocks you want to buy and at what prices. If you do not have such a list, just buy one or more ETFs.

For starters, just trade ETFs and you can skip the latter chapters in evaluating stocks.

In the simplest terms, I discussed how to evaluate stocks fundamentally and technically. Use the research available in the free sites such as finviz.com. Instead of spending hours in researching one stock, you can do the same in a few minutes as others have researched them for you.

Many of my other books are mentioned for future references. You do not need to read them now unless you want to further your education in investing. Actually this book provides a lot of information including the entire bonus section for more advanced study. When you have mastered the techniques in this book, try out "Complete The Art of Investing" described in Appendix 2.

I am not a writer but a retail investor similar to most of you. I've been making a comfortable living via my investment ideas that I'm sharing in this book.

Some of the strategies described here have been used in my book Best Stocks 2014, According to Me. From 12/16/13 (the publish date) to 3/4/14, the list of all 135 selected stocks beat SPY (an ETF simulating the S&P 500) by 103% and the list of 9 small cap stocks beat SPY by 500% without considering dividends and compounding.

Retail investors have a lot of advantages over fund managers. However, I advise not to be a trader especially day traders for beginners. Statistically most amateur traders lose money as they cannot compete with experienced, disciplined traders. Even if you study several good books by great traders, most likely you will still lose money initially. No books can replace the actual trading experience.

For beginner investors
Both Fidelity and AAII (both require being a client or a member) have excellent articles for beginners. Alternatively, buy a book for beginners. To include all the basic terms and concepts, I have to double the size of this book which is already lengthy and bore most readers who already have the basic knowledge.

Click here for Morningstar classroom.
http://morningstar.com/cover/classroom.html

Click here for Fidelity basic in investing.
https://www.fidelity.com/investment-guidance/investing-basics

How this book is organized
Most graphs are in landscape orientation for both paperback and e-readers. Some graphs may not be displayed adequately on a small screen of an e-reader. E-readers may be available in the current version of Windows, so you can read e-books on the larger screen of your PC. For better orientation, just flip the e-readers 90 degrees.

A link is usually included for these screens. Copy it to your browser to display the graphs on your PC if desirable. Instructions on how to produce some graphs are provided as you should try them out. One example is how to produce a chart on detecting market crashes.

It is easier to display some tables in landscape mode, which can be selected in your e-reader. Select a table or a graph via your e-reader to display it to fit the screen.

The font size and page size of most e-book formats can be adjusted. The unknown, special character is the "smiling face" that the current Kindle does not convert correctly as of this writing.

There are clickable links to web articles. Most of them are from my own web sites and public web sites such as Wikipedia. Some public links may not be available in the future as they are not under my control.

Fidelity Video provides video clips to explain some basic terms and it may require Fidelity customers to sign on in order to view them. Check the trial offer from Fidelity. YouTube offers similar video lessons.

These links extend the usefulness of this book by making available specific topics that may not be interesting to every reader.

The current version provides most of the links the paperback readers can enter into your browser. Get the same information by entering a search in Wikipedia such as Dogs of Dow.

Investopedia is another source beside Wikipedia.
http://www.investopedia.com/

'Afterthoughts' includes my additional comments and comments from others. Readers can make comments in this book's website.

There are fillers with tips and jokes to fill up the empty space of the printed book.

For convenience, this book uses SPY, an Exchange Traded Fund (ETF) simulating the S&P 500, as the benchmark for the market.

Annualized returns (Return * 365 / (Days between)) are used where appropriate for more meaningful comparison. To illustrate, I have a 10% return in 6 months, a 10% in a year and a 10% in 2 years. It is more meaningful to use annualized returns of 20%, 10% and 5% respectively for the 6-month return, the one-year return and the 2-year return in this example.

Usually I do not include the dividend, so you can add an estimated 1.5% to the annualized return. In addition, compound interest is not used for easier calculation, so the actual return could be even better.

About the author
I graduated from Cal. State University at San Jose in Industrial Engineering and University of Mass. in Amherst with a MS in Industrial Engineering. I have been an investor for over 30 years.

Dedication
To all retail investors and future retail investors including my grandchildren.

AcknowledgementThanks to: Seeking Alpha, Wikipedia and Investopedia for the many helpful links to enrich this book. Yahoo!Finance and Finviz.com for the tools and charts used in this book. Poi for gathering my research info and working on the business side of the9 book.

Important notices
© 2014-17 Tony Pow

Version	Paperback	eBooks
1.00	05/14	05/14
1.11	09/17	09/17

Printed version of ISBN-13 978-1499190502 or ISBN-10: 1499190506. No part of this book can be reproduced in any form without the written approval of the author.

Disclaimer

Do not gamble money that you cannot afford to lose. Past performance is a guideline and is not necessarily indicative of future results. All information is believed to be accurate, but there it is not guaranteed. All the strategies described have no guarantee that they will make money and they may lose money. Do not trade without doing due diligence and be warned that most data would be obsolete. All my articles and the associated data are for informational and illustration purposes only. I'm not a professional investment counselor or a tax professional. Seek one before you make any investment decision. The above mentioned also applies for all other advice such as on accounting, taxes, health and any topic mentioned in this book. I am not a professional in any of these fields. Same for all the links contained in this book. Some articles may offend some one or some organization unintentionally. If I did, I'm sorry about that. I am politically and religiously neutral. I try my best effort to ensure the accuracy of my articles. Data also from different sources was believed to be accurate. However, there is no guarantee that they are accurate and suitable for the current market conditions and /or your individual situations. My publisher and I are not liable for any damages in using this book.

Filler:

A joke: a nightmare or reality

I got a call from Buffett asking me to lead their stock research. I asked him why for a nobody; you may be asking the same question. No kidding.

He told me that he should have read my book Scoring Stocks to buy Apple instead of IBM in May, 2013. It would save his company millions of dollars minus $10 for my book. Not to mention the market timing technique that had worked in the last two major market plunges.

I told him, "OK, I'll beat your mediocre returns of the last 5 years." He said, "You can do better than that and at least beat SPY. If you do so, no one will be that stupid to leave my fund and pay the hefty capital gain taxes."

I told him, "I cannot beat the market as you are the market especially after your expensive fees. In addition, I do not know how to avoid day traders from riding my wagon in trading. Also most of my big profits were made in small stocks that your fund cannot trade besides owning the company." I woke up trembling. I'm glad it is only a nightmare.

I Market timing on market crashes

The apples you picked are sour but some other times are tasty from the same tree. You just pick them in the wrong time or in the right time. It is nothing wrong with the tree but timing.

Market timing is about educated guesses unless you have a time machine ☺. Hopefully we will have more rights than wrongs when we follow general guidelines. It would reduce risk and could benefit us financially in the long run.

I divide the market timing in three categories by durations as follows. All time durations are estimates.

1. Secular Cycle.   Duration: 20 years.
2. Market Cycle.   Duration: 5 years.
3. Correction.   Duration: 6 months.

A useful table for the parameters in the next chapters

If SMA-350% (Simple Moving Average for last 350 trade sessions) is zero, exit the market. It means the market (represented by SPY, an ETF for S&P 500) moves below its moving average (350 days).

Afterwards, when it is above zero, reenter the market.

We use SMA-200 as it is readily available from finviz.com.

	SMA-350	SMA-50	SMA-200	SMA50/SMA200	RSI (14)
Market					
Peak	9%		5%	101%	65%
Bottom	-31%		-32%	78%	25%
Correction					
Peak	8%	3%	4%	102%	68%
Bottom	-7%	-5%	-8%	97%	26%
Stock					
Peak					70%
Bottom					30%

1   Simplest market timing

Market timing depends on charts; the following describes how to use chart information without creating charts. Most charts will not identify the peaks and bottoms of the market as they depend on data (i.e. the stock prices). However, it would reduce further loses.

It is simpler than it sounds. Just follow the following procedure.

How

The first part of this technique detects market plunges and the second part advises reentry to the market.

How to detect market plunges without charts (a.k.a. Death Cross)

1. Bring up Finviz.com.

2. Enter SPY (or any ETF that simulates the market).

3. If SMA-200% is positive, it indicates that market plunging has not been detected and you can skip the following steps.

4. The market is plunging if SMA-50% is more negative than SMA-200%. To illustrate this condition, SMA-200% is -2% and SMA-50% is -5%.

5. Sell most stocks starting with the riskiest ones first such as the ones with high P/Es and/or high Debt/Equity. Obtain this info from Finviz.com by entering the symbol of the stock you own.

6. For the conservative investors, sell those over-priced stocks only. For aggressive investors, sell all stocks. For the extreme aggressive ones, buy contra ETFs besides selling all stocks.

When to return to the market (a.k.a. Golden Cross)

Use the above in a reversed sense to detect whether the market has been recovering. However, when the SMA-200% is positive, I would start buying value stocks (low P/E but the 'E' has to be positive and/or low Debt/Equity).

1. Bring up Finviz.com.

2. Enter SPY (or any ETF that simulates the market).

3. If SMA-200% is negative, the market is not recovering according to this indicator and you can skip the following steps.

4. Start buying the best value stocks. Sell all contra ETFs if you have any. You can re-evaluate the stocks from my list of my other book Best Stocks for 20XX. I should have a book when the market is favorable for buying stocks, but it is not a promise.

5. Market recovery is confirmed when SMA-50% is more positive than SMA-200%. To illustrate this condition, SMA-200% is 2% and SMA-50% is 5%. Commit larger percent (or all for aggressive investors) of your cash to stocks.

Do the above once a month. When the SPY price is closer to SMA actions percentage, perform the above once a week.

The charts and data for market timing described in this book are based on SMA-350 that is more preferred than this simple procedure without using charts.

Note.

Predictions are predictions. However, the more the educated the guess is, the better chance the guess will materialize. It does not mean it will always materialize as the market changes and sometimes it is not rational.

My technical indicator (SMA-350) gave only one false alarm from 2000 to 2010. False signals happen more often after this period. The market is far more volatile than before. In most cases, false alarms will not hurt at all except the tax consequences on taxable accounts. The false alarm tells us to exit the market and come back to the market shortly.

II Market correction

Market corrections are harder to detect compared to market crashes. However, it would save you a lot.

2 Do

Technical indicators may detect whether the market is ripe for temporary dips. I estimate there are about two dips a year for illustration only as this number fluctuates every year. If the price is far away from the SMA, it may be peaking. RSI(14), the relative strength index using last 14 days, determines whether the stock is overbought.

It is not always reliable. However, exiting from the temporary peak would make you more money. Here are our 'do's.

1. Bring up finviz.com from your browser.

2. Enter SPY (an ETF simulating S&P 500) on "Search Ticket".

3. SMA-200, Single Moving Average for 200 days, is in the bottom line of the metrics.

4. It indicates how far away is the current stock price from the SMA-200.

5. The market is peaking when SMA-200 is over 5%.

6. RSI(14) can be located in the right hand side of the metrics.

7. The market is overbought when RSI(14) is over 65%.

8. Actions:

    1. Do not buy stocks including ETFs when a correction is expected as indicated by these two conditions.

    2. Do not want to exit the market totally as the market still could head higher.

    3. Sell some stocks that have reached your objectives. Do not sell more than 25% of your portfolio.

4. Set stop loss on the remaining stocks you bought. Recommend to use 5% less than the current prices and 10% for volatile stocks. Adjust the stops accordingly every month.

5. If you trade SPY or other ETFs stocks instead of stocks, you can go back to your couch.

    If not, prepare a list of stocks to buy. My book Best Stocks 2014, According to me or the later book in this series provide you with a list of stocks.

6. When the correction materializes, buy the ETFs and/or the stocks you prepared for. If the correction is 5%, buy the stocks at 5% off (individual stocks vary in the suggested 5%).

7. A lot of time, the correction does not happen shortly, go back to step #1.

The above is very similar to detecting the market peaking as described except with the thresholds of SMA-200% and RSI(14). Do the above once a month. When SPY is closer to its SMA action percent, perform the above once a week.

The next chapters in this section are for the details. It would be too heavy for beginners but it will be handy for future reference.

So far you may have already opened the first chest of knowledge and can go back to your couch.

The next section describes how to take advantage of the calendar in investing. After this, the next sections describe how to evaluate stocks fundamentally and technically with minimal effort.

III Market timing by calendar

Some periods are more favorable than others statistically. They do not always work as predicted, so do not commit more than 25%.

3 Do

I made the following charts so it is easier to time the market by calendar. All dates are inclusive.

No.	Metric		Score
1	Seasonal	Nov. - April, Score = 1	
2	Best Month	Nov., Score = 1	
		Sep., Score = -1	
3	Best Days	Dec. 15 – Jan.15 Score = 1	
4	Presidential Cycle	Election Year, Score = 1	
		1st Year in Office, Score = -1	
		2nd year, Score = -1	
		3rd year, Score = 2	
		Early Recovery, Score = 3	
		Up, Score = 2	
		Peak, Score = 1	
		SMA200% > 6%[2] Score = -1	
		RSI(14) > 65% Score = -1	
6	Presidential[3]	Democratic = 1 Republican = -1	
		Grand Score	

Footnote.

[1] Refer to Market Cycle chapter on how I define phases of a cycle.

[2] For simplicity, use finviz.com. Enter SPY and you will find SMA200% and RSI(14) to predict whether the market is peaking and overbought.

[3] I'm political neutral. The selection is based on historical statistics.

Add up all the scores. The passing grade is 0. According to my table which is based on my personal selections, the market is favorable when the grand score is 1 or higher. I bet it is the first time you see such a scoring system combing with market timing.

Sectors for market cycle

Market Phase[1]	Favorable	Unfavorable
Early Recovery	Financial, Technology, Industrial	Energy, Telecom, Utilities
Up	Technology, Industrial	
Peak	Mineral, Health Care, Energy	
Bottom	Consumer Staples, Utilities	Consumer Discretionary, Technology, Industrial
Seasonal	**Favorable**	**Unfavorable**
Winter	Energy, Utilities	
End of year	QQQ, EWG	
Olympics	ETF for host country[2]	

Footnote.

[1] Refer to Market Cycle chapter on how I define phases of a cycle.

[2] Buy it next year after Olympics. It could be due to higher GDP or the publicity. However, be selective. Greece is too small a country to host an Olympics.

IV Finding Stocks

4 Finviz's screener

We can use the fundamental screen described and then evaluate stocks using technical indicators. Alternatively, use your favorite screener with the same concepts described next for each of the three strategies.

Finviz.com provides a screening incorporating both fundamental and technical metrics and is one of the best free sites. Bring up finviz.com in your browser and select screener. You have 4 tabs: Descriptive, Fundamental, Technical and All.

Besides incorporating technical indicators, it has the following features:

- The criteria specified can be saved.

- The searched stocks can be saved in a portfolio (for paper test and performance monitor).

- For extra fee, you can have historical database (I have not tested this feature to comment).

- Some advanced technical indicators such as Candlestick (very useful as a momentum indicator).

However, it lacks the following features:

- Stocks with prices trending up in the last several weeks (such as increasing X% in previous week and y% in week before the previous week, etc.).

- Using exponential moving averages that have better predictive power than simple moving averages for momentum investing. Selecting ranges (for example, it cannot select all three major exchanges, market cap ranges, etc.).

Common selection criteria

- Avg. Volume. If the stock price is less than $10, change it to ">200K".

- If you have found a lot of stocks, enter more fundamental criteria.

- If you have found too few stocks, relax the criteria.

- Do not trust the financial data of small companies esp. foreign companies.

- Buy the stock on uptrend (200 SMA). It stands for Single Moving Average for the last 200 trade sessions.

- RSI(14) indicates whether the stock is overbought.

- Evaluate the stock.

- Read articles on the stock. Try SeekingAlpha to start. Your broker may have articles from analysts.

Picture filler:

V Research stock by fundamentals

5 Do

Many stocks have already been researched. Most are available to us free of charge. I start with five free sites as described in the link, followed by Blue Chip Growth and my simple scoring system. If you are a customer of Fidelity, try out their Analyst Opinions.

Several sources

The popular ones are Morningstar, Value Line, The Street and Zacks. If they are not available free, check out whether they are available from your library.

Blue Chip Growth

Click here for Blue Chip Growth which is free currently for stock analysis. To illustrate, enter IBM as the stock symbol. As of 2/2013, it gives C for a Total Grade, D for Quantity Grade and B for Fundamental Grade. The Total Grade is a composite grade of other grades. If the Total Grade and the Fundamental Grade are A or B, the stock most likely is good.

http://navelliergrowth.investorplace.com/bluechip

A simple scoring system

Bring up Finviz.com and then enter the stock symbol.

No.	Metric	Good	Bad	Score
1	Forward P/E[1]	Between 2.5 and 12.5, Score = 2	> 50 or < 0, Score = -1	
2	P/ FCF[1]	< 12, Score = 1	>30 or < 0, Score = -1	
3	P/S[1]	< 0.8, Score = 1	< 0, Score = -1	
4	P/ B[1]	< 1, Score = 1	< 0, Score = -1	
	Compare quarter to quarter of last			

		year			
5	Sales Q/Q	> 15%, Score = 1	< 0, Score = -1	
6	EPS Q/Q	> 20%, Score = 1	< 0, Score = -1	
			Grand Score	
	Stock Symbol Date²	Current Price	SPY	

Footnote.
1. Negative values for Sales (due to accounting adjustments), Equity and Book are possible but not likely.
2. The last row is for your information only. SPY is used to measure whether it will beat the market by comparing the return of this stock to the return of SPY.

The Score

Score each metric and sum up all the scores giving the Grand Score. If the Grand Score is 3, the stock passes this scoring system. Even if it is a 2, it still deserves further analysis if you have time. You may want to add scores from other vendors. To illustrate using Blue Chip Growth, add 1 for score A and -1 for score F.

Other sources

If you have other sources (most require subscription or being a customer), skip the stocks with one of the failing grades. Ignore them if there is new positive development such as increased insider purchases.

Vendor	Grade	Fail
Fidelity	Analysts' Opinions	< 4
IBD	Composite	< 50
Value Line	Proj. 3-5 yrs. Return	< 3%
Zacks	Rank	5
Vector Vest	VST	< 0.7

You may be able to find them from the library. Try out the free stock reports from your broker. Seeking Alpha has articles on stocks and earnings conferences, which could have important information after separating from the "welcome" and garbage talks.

Very basic advices for beginners

They are Market Cap (capitalization), Debt/Equity and P/E. For beginners, stick with U.S. stocks with Market Cap greater than 800 M (million), Debt/Equity less than .25 (25%) except for debt-intensive industries such as utilities and airlines and P/E between 5 to 20. These metrics are available from Finviz.com.

Do not have more than 20% of your portfolio in one stock and do not have more than 30% of your portfolio in one sector.

Do not buy stocks if they are not A or B in both the composite grade and the fundamental grade from Blue Chip Growth.

For more conservative investors, use beta (available from Yahoo!Finance) less than 1. Beta of 1 represents the market (S&P 500 index). For example, a stock with beta 1.5 statistically fluctuates more than 50% of the market.

Try virtual trading (i.e. trade stocks without real money) to check out your strategy and your skill in trading stocks. If your broker does not provide one, use a spreadsheet to record your trades or simulator.investopedia.com.

Fundamental metrics

ROE

Return of equity (ROE) could be the most important financial indicator to determine how well the management is doing the job. However, in recent years, this metric has been over-used and it loses its reliability in prediction.

The company's return on equity for at least the last five years would indicate how the stock price endures major financial downturns as well as upturns.

Comparing the ROE to the average ROE for the sector is a good indicator on how well the company is managed compared to its peers. Some sectors including utilities have low average ROEs.

Market Cap (Capitalization)

Market Cap = Total no. of outstanding shares * share price

For beginners, I recommend to buy U.S. stocks with market cap greater than 800 M (million). Here are the current conventions (everyone's convention is different) and they should be adjusted to inflation.

Class	Market Cap (million)
Nano Cap	< $50M
Micro Cap	$50M to $250M
Small Cap	$250M to $1B (billion)
Mid Cap	$1B to $10B
Large Cap (Blue Chip)	$10B to $50B
Mega Cap	>50B

The higher the cap is, the less risky is the stock. Nano Cap and Micro Cap are reserved for speculators or owners of the companies. Small Cap and Mid Cap are for knowledgeable investors as most institutional investors would skip the stocks in these caps especially Small Cap. Large Cap, Mega Cap and some Mid Cap are the stocks traded by institutional investors. They are thoroughly researched continuously.

My metrics
My current favorites are Expected P/E, PEG, Analysts' Opinions, Short % of outstanding shares, Free Cash Flow, ROE and Debt Load / Equity.

In addition, I use many summarized metrics from different sources. For example, one of my subscription services gives me a composite rank for fundamentals and another one for momentum. To illustrate, click here for Blue Chip Growth which is free currently for stock analysis. Enter IBM as the stock symbol. As of 2/2013, it gives C for a Total Grade, D for Quantity Grade and B for Fundamental Grade. The Total Grade is usually a composite grade of other grades.

Use the metrics to screen through the stocks to reduce the number of stocks for further consideration. After being burnt several times by small Chinese companies, I just skip most of them.

Mid, high and low values of common metrics

Metric	Mid Range	Low Range	High Range
P/E (last 12 months)	< 10	>40	< 4
Price / Cash Flow	< 12	>30	< 4
Price / Sales	< 2.5	>3	< .2
Price / Book	< 2.0	>4	< .2
PEG	< 1.5	>2	< .2

High Range means good values (although in this table it means low numbers), but sometimes it is too good to be true. Low Range means bad values. To illustrate, many internet stocks in 2000 had P/E over 40 (bad) while a neglected bargain stock has a P/E of 3 (supposed to be good). A bargain could also mean there could have some hidden problem. In reality, I prefer the Mid Range. Using P/E to illustrate, it should be between 4 and 10. Adjust the range according to your personal tolerance and the current market conditions. If the market trend is up, you may want to relax the range to 5 to 12 for example otherwise you cannot find too many stocks for further evaluation.

These values are my selections based on data for about 10 years. They are used for prediction the performance of a stock in a year; check the ranges every 6 months in the current market.

The metrics with high-range and mid-range values offer better prediction for stock price appreciation. From the above table, the stocks with low-range values have a better chance than other stocks to lose money in a year or so. Some favorable numbers could be high values instead of low values such as ROE.

However, the range values could change. When the market favors momentum or you do not keep stocks for less than a month or so, the momentum metrics including PEG and price growth could be better predicators. We need to check whether the current market favors which group of the metrics: Value or Growth – some web sites and subscription services identify the current favorite. In addition, the performance of each metric should be evaluated every 3 to 6 months. In addition, new range values need to be adjusted to in the above table.

Fundamental metrics take a longer time (about 6-12 months vs. 1 month for momentum metrics) for the performance to materialize. The metrics in the above table beside PEG are all fundamental metrics. Except for financial stocks, P/B is always worthless.

Example of searching with high range values

Stocks with low-range values for most metrics (such as 40 in P/E in the above table) could be risky. Hence, select the stocks with the mid-range value (e.g. 10 for P/E). Avoid the low-range values indicated by the metrics.

Here is one example of selecting stocks with high range values of P/E and P/B. Most likely, you cannot find too many stocks with these criteria.

$E > 0$ and
$P/E < 4$ and
$P/B < .2$

E is earning per share and we need the company to be profitable.

High range values could indicate something wrong with the company, e.g. a lawsuit pending. I would consider a P/E of less than 4 is suspicious. However, very small companies are often neglected by the market, so they could be solid companies. Don't forget to do your due diligence and spend more time in thoroughly evaluating the stock and its industry.

The stocks with low-range values have a greater chance to lose money in the next year or so. That is proven statistically as a group despite some exceptions. AMZN[2] is not a valued stock by its high P/E or its high P/B. However, if the company is investing for the future by building infrastructure and capturing market share, you may ignore these unfavorable metrics. Personally I prefer fundamentally sound companies today.

Note. P/B is not a good metric for established companies and / or companies with a lot of research such as IBM. Many metric formulae are outdated due to ignoring intellectual properties, patents and market appeals such as brand names.\

Example of a search for mid-range values

E > 0 and
P/E < 10 and
P/E > 4

In this case, you only include companies with positive earnings and P/Es within the range from 4 to 10 exclusively. You should find many companies with the mid-range values of P/Es.

Add other filters such as minimum price, market cap and average volume. If you do not find too many stocks, relax your criteria (start with mid-range values in the table), and vice versa to limit the number of stocks. If you find stocks usually with a screen but not today, it usually means that the market is over-valued that you cannot find many bargain stocks.

Again, it is the first step to narrow down the number of stocks to be analyzed. Your metrics will not cover stocks with special situations. For example, IBM always has a high Price/Book value as long as I can remember and it does not mean it should be excluded.

The searches based on fundamental metrics help us to narrow stocks for further evaluations. Occasionally I abandon the scoring system for some stocks under special conditions.

Compare company's metrics to its sector averages[1]

This could be the most powerful comparison: Compare Apples to Apples.

You may want to compare the metrics of a company to the averages of that sector. The average of supermarket's P/S is extremely low and hence it has no meaning to compare a supermarket's P/S to most other sectors. Some sectors like utilities need high debt to run a utility company.

However, when the average P/E or other metric of a sector is suddenly lower than its historical average, it could mean that sector is out-of-favor and/or the sector is having better value.

This following table compares Apple to its sector and a retail sector on a specific date for illustration. All the metrics will change.

Metric	Apple	Computer	Retail
P/E	11	19	24
(5 year average)	16	17	15
PEG	.6	N/A	1.4
Price /Cash Flow	9.4	8.1	9.2
Price /Book	3.3	3.0	3.6
EPS Growth	-6%	-42%	2.6%
(last 5 years)	62%	45%	11%
Operating Margin	20%	15%	8%
ROE	30%	14%	19%
Debt / Equity	2%	7%	88%
Inventory Turnover	76%	53%	4.55x

From the above table, some metrics only make sense for an industrial sector (Computer for Apple). In this case, you want to compare AAPL to Computer, and not to Retail.

"Debt / Equity" indicates that the retail sector needs to borrow more than computer sector for example. So is Inventory Turnover.

Top down approach

First, compare whether the market is risky. Second, select the best sector; there are many sites including Finviz.com to select the best sector. Then compare the fundamental metrics of the major stocks within that sector.

Some metrics do not apply

Using financial institutions as an example, usually P/B is more useful than P/CF. However, the quality of loan (not a metric here) is more important than all metrics as we found out in 2007. P/S is more important for retails. However, the expected P/E is most important for most other sectors.

When you believe a sector is best currently, select stocks only for this sector, a criterion available in many screeners.

Compare metrics to its five-year average

If the company's five-year average of P/E is 20 and today it is 10. It is 100% under-valued by this standard. Try other metrics such as debt/equity.

Growth Metrics

The growth metrics are growth rates of the stock price, sales, earnings, etc. They are useful for growth investors.

Even for value investors, earning growth rate is very important, as most stocks with substantial gains have increased their earnings growth first. If the earning has grown but the price remains the same (i.e. PEG), then the potential for price appreciation will be higher and most likely it will return to the historical average P/E.

Momentum Metrics

Momentum metrics is part of growth. The rates of increase of the stock price, the volume... are the major metrics. Earnings revision is another one especially in earning announcement seasons (4 times a year). Many subscription services provide a composite rank with name Timely or similar name. In my momentum portfolio, I use these metrics and ignore all other metrics as my average holding period is less than 30 days for momentum strategy.

Insiders' buying

Insiders sell their stocks for many reasons. When insiders buy a lot of their companies' stocks at market prices, take notice. Insiders know better than anyone about the health of their companies and their industries.

Select Insiders' purchases from one of the available sites such as Finviz.com. Ignore the option exercises. I prefer the high ratios of Net Total Purchase Value / Market Cap and the purchases by more than one insider. Be careful that the insider did not purchase the stocks after selling similar amount of stock.

OpenInsider is a good site for this info.

InsiderSights is a good one too with more capable tools that would take more time to learn.

Where to get the metrics

You can get this information from the web site with no or low cost such as Finviz.com, your broker's site, AAII (very low cost) and Blue Chip Growth (free so far).

The following subscriptions are at a little higher cost but they are still less than $1,000 per year: Value Line, IBD, Zacks, Vector Vest and Stock Screen 123. Many data from different vendors are duplicated. You will save time by concentrating on one or two sources.

Many vendors provide a composite metric such as a value metric to cover P/E, debt... and a timing metric to cover Technical Analysis indicators, PEG, price appreciation rate...

Short % is a useful metric available in Finviz.com. For Fidelity customers, you can click on Research and then Stock. Enter the stock name, and then click on Detailed. I find Fidelity's Analysts' Opinions quite useful.

Finviz.com provides a lot of useful information free of charge. It also provides a screen function. The 'Help' button describes Finviz's functions and all the metrics monitored.

Other sources are: Insider Cow, NASDAQ Guru Analysis ...

Monitor the recent performance of the metrics

The predictability of most metrics has proven not to perform consistently as many investors and fund managers found it out. My theory is that the specific metric works better in some market conditions than others. To test which ones work better currently, check their performance in the last three months and use those that perform well. This is my scoring system in the book Scoring Stocks is based on.

Why some metrics fail sometimes

Most investors are using metrics to screen stocks, but few are successful consistently. Some investment companies have top analysts dedicated to projects looking for the right strategy. My guess why they fail:

1. Metrics need to be monitored to see its effectiveness on current market conditions.

2. Besides fundamental metrics, there are many intangibles.

3. When they have too many followers on the same metrics, they will not work such as ROE in last several years.

4. Fundamentals need time (at least 6 months) to reflect the value of the stock. You're swimming against the tide as a fundamentalist. Trading momentum stocks using basic fundamentals will not work.

5. Watch out 'Garbage in and garbage out'. Some emerging countries do not have organization similar to SEC to ensure the integrity of the financial statements of a company and some audit firms are being paid to cover their eyes. Even there are frauds in some U.S. companies and their auditors.

6. The metrics are derived from obsolete financial statements. Check out the date. The most updated one could be available from the company's website.

7. Some companies borrow a lot of money to dress up the metrics such as P/E and ROE. They will look good short-term but not long-term. Ensure the debt/equity has not been increased recently for this purpose. I recall one utility spin-off has incredible fundamentals except the debt load. It is so high that all these fundamentals will deteriorate in the future due to servicing its high debts.

Footnote

[1] The stocks are classified into sector and then sub classified into industries. For example, oil is a sector and oil exploration and oil services are industries under the oil sector. For simplicity, I intermix

the terms here as many sectors do not need further sub classifications for this discussion.

[2] AMZN is not a value stock by any standard. As of 1/1/2013, its P/E (from last 12 months) is 157 and P/B is 15. Both fall far into my low-range values. Its price rises from 256 from 1/1/13 to 270 today (1/22/13). Today its P/E is ridiculously over 3,000. The investors are betting AMZN's internet sales will take over the concrete stores and its investors do not care about profit but for market share. Does it sound like familiar in the internet era? Its price momentum is indicated positively by any chart. It may be a good stock for traders, but it is too risky for a swing trader and a long-term investor like me (yes, I wear two hats). I do not short stocks in a rising market, but this could be an exception.

Afterthoughts

- The only recommendation from a very popular investment book to select stocks is the return of equity (ROE). I will save you the time and money to read that book. I read the entire book in an hour at Barnes and Noble's and it saved me some money / time, not to mention cutting down trees for that book. Basically it does not work today.
- DAL has an interesting Debt / Equity of over -1000% due to the negative equity. For a comparison, you may want to use Debt / ABS(Equity).

- Once in a while, I found the financial data are not consistent from different sources. Try to check out any discrepancy in the dates of the financial data of the sources. The financial statements from the company websites usually have the most updated data.

- <u>Current Ratio</u> = Current Asset / Current Liability. If it is below 1, then the company is having a tough time to meeting its current cash obligation.

- Dividend Yield is a valid metric for matured companies. I do not use it to evaluate growth companies or companies that need to plow back cash for research and development.

- If you use Finviz.com, you find three margins: profit, gross and operating. I prefer to use profit margin that is more useful to compare companies in different sectors.

  http://www.investopedia.com/terms/p/profitmargin.asp
  http://www.investopedia.com/terms/g/grossmargin.asp
  http://www.investopedia.com/terms/o/operatingmargin.asp

  Use Wikipedia for more description.

- Enron had millions in profits but negative cash flows. Earnings can be manipulated but not the cash flows.

  Insiders' selling usually does not cause any alarm unless excessively. Most insiders sell most of the stocks they have before these companies bankrupt. Just common sense!

- Why fundamentals are important.
  (http://seekingalpha.com/article/1612442-its-shorting-season)

  On the same day when this article was published, RVLT was up 10% due to increasing sales on the earnings conference. However, the company is still not profitable. It shows how tough is shorting even with good arguments.

- Due to my ignorance, limited time or my short period of holding stocks, I have not used intrinsic value that often.

  Book value is different from intrinsic value. Book value is calculated by summing up the values of all pieces of a company such as a building and a machine.

  Intrinsic value is the real value of a company. When two companies have the same book value and market cap, the company that generates more profit than the other one usually has higher intrinsic value. When the intrinsic value is higher than the stock price, it is underpriced in theory.

  The following link provides more info on intrinsic value.
  http://en.wikipedia.org/wiki/Intrinsic_value_%28finance%29

Finviz parameters

Most metrics are described in Finviz (via Help), Investopedia and/or Wikipedia and the chapter on P/E. The following are my personal comments and why some metrics are more important than others. Compare the ratios to the companies in the same sector and also its averages from the last 5 years.

Also, they are roughly based on the flow of Finviz skipping those metric I believe not too important. You can also place your cursor on the metric to have the description from Finviz. Some metrics are left blank when they are zero or negative.

- **Index**. Usually we use Exchange. Most of us trade stocks in the three major exchanges in the USA. Stocks listed over-the-counter are too risky to many. Skip the stocks in local exchanges and foreign exchanges if you are not an expert on these stocks.

- **Market Cap** (MC). To me, stocks below 50M are risky even they could be very profitable. Ensure the Avg. Volume is at least 10,000 shares or your order is less 1% of the average volume. Some small stocks are controlled by the owners with small volumes. In this case you cannot sell your stock easily.

  Float = Outstanding shares – Insider shares.
  Usually it does not matter as they are typically the same. However, it does for small companies with large insider shares. Most of these owners do not want to sell their family businesses and hence they reduce the chance of being acquired entirely or partly for good prices.

- If **Expected P/E** is not provided, use the P/E which is based on the last 12 months. Alternatively, calculate the E by using the E from P/E and multiplying it by its growth rate. It may not be seasonally adjusted. I prefer Expected P/E (or called Forward P/E) as it has better predictability power from my limited research.

- **Cash / share**. It is used to calculate Pow P/E and Pow EY. To illustrate, if the stock is $10 and it has $10 cash / share without debt (i.e. Debt/Equity = 0), most likely it is underpriced as you can get the whole company for nothing. You should find out why the price is so low.

- **Dividend %** is useful for income investors. The payout ratio should not be more than 30% except for matured companies.

- **Recs**. Select stocks with 1 or 2. Do not base on their recommendation alone. There have been many bad recommendations that would cost you a fortune.

    If your broker is Fidelity, use their Analysts' Opinion. It is based on the previous performances of the analysts. Just for this feature alone, I recommend opening an account with minimum requirements — I do not get any compensation from them. Also, it would spare you from reading 30 or so pages on this topic that I believe it is a waste of time.

- **PEG** is a measure of the growth of P/E and hence a growth metric. The lower, the better. If there are two companies with the same P/E, the one with better PEG is better. EPS Growth is similar metric with Earnings. I prefer PEG over EPS growth. If two companies have the same E/P, the Earnings Growth (EPS Q/Q) would be the tie breaker.

- **P/B**. Book value (= Total Assets − Total Liabilities) may not include intangible asset such as patents. Do not trust it 100%, so is ROE which is based on book value. Negative equity is possible when Total Liabilities is more than Total Assets.

- **P/FCF**. I prefer it greater than 0 and less than 50 for value investors.

- **Sales Q/Q** reduces the seasonal deviation. To illustrate, retail sales for Christmas season should compare it to same season in prior year.

- **EPS Q/Q**. Same as above. I prefer the growth of EPS over Sales. The Q/Q ratios are growth metrics. When a company terminates its unprofitable product(s), its Sales Q/Q could be down but its EPS Q/Q could be up. In 2000, many internet companies had great Sales Q/Qs but negative EPS Q/Qs.

When the company buys its own shares, EPS could be misleading as E is fixed and the number of shares is reduced.

- **Profit Margin.** I prefer it over Gross Margin and Oper. Margin which does not include interest expenses and taxes. When you sell software, the Gross Margin is high as it does not include development, support and marketing, etc. A retail store has low Gross Margin.

- **Short Float.** I prefer it less than 10%. If it is greater than 10%, the shorters could find something wrong with the company. If it is over 25%, I would check the fundamentals. If they are good, I buy it betting on a short squeeze. It has been risky but proven to be profitable to me.

- Technical metrics: **SMA-20**, SMA-50 and SMA-200. If they are all positive, it means the trend is good. SMA-20 is short-term trend and SMA-200 is long-term trend. If you are short-term swing investor, stick with short-term trend and vice versa.

- **RSI(14)**. If it greater than 60% (some use 65%), it is overbought. If it is under 30% (some use 25%), it is under bought. Use it as a reference. Most stocks making new heights are always overbought.

- Management performance is measured by ROA. It is also judged by Analysts' Rec. and Inst Own (except for small companies). The confidence of their own ability, the company and its sector is measured by Insider Own and Insider Purchase.

- Avoid all bankrupting companies at all cost. Debt/Equity, P/FCF, Cash/Sh., P/B, Profit Margin, Forward P/E, Short Float, RSI(14), SMA20% and SMA50 would give us hints. Need to summarize all the info and study many other factors such as obsoleting products (including drugs).

More useful information:

- The price chart. It has a lot of features such as the resistance line. Some charts include technical indicators such as double top (a bearish warning) and double bottom (a bullish sign).

- Description under the symbol. It briefly describes what the company (sector and industry) does and its country of registration. You want to buy a stock in a sector in its uptrend. Industry is a sub sector. For example according to Finviz, Apple is in Consumer Goods sector and Electronic Equipment industry. If you do not want to buy foreign stocks, skip it if it is not listed in the US exchange.
- Articles on the company.
- Insider trading. Pay more attention to the insider purchases at market prices. Use common sense.
- Groups helps you to determine whether the stock is in a sector trending up.

Summary

The following improves the odd of success but there is no guarantee.

Risky Market?

Bring up Finviz.com. Enter SPY. If both SMA-50% and SMA-200% are both negative, do not invest especially when SMA-50% is more negative than SMA-200%.

Evaluation value stocks from others' research

Gather a list of stocks from screens and/or recommendations from magazines. Use researches that are available. Value stocks should be kept for at least 6 months and do another evaluation then. There are many other free sources such as IBD, GuruFocus, Zacks and MorningStar.

Name	Pass Grade	Link[1]
Blue Chip Growth[2]	Total = A or B	Link
	Fund = A or B	
Vector Vest[3]	VST > 1 and RV > 1	Link
Value Line[4]	Timeliness > Average	
	Proj. 3-5 yr% > 5%	
Fidelity Analyst Opinion	>5	Customer

1   Links. Just Google the Name and select the web site.
2   Currently free.
3   Free for limited number of stocks and free trial.
4   Should be available from your local library.

Evaluate stocks

Bring up Finviz.com and enter the stock symbol.

Metric	Passing Grade
Forward P/E	Between 5 and 15
P/FCF	< 15 and ratio is positive
Sales Q/Q	>10
EPS Q/Q	>15

Intangible Analysis

Bring up Seeking Alpha and enter the stock symbol. To prevent manipulation, only use it for stocks with larger cap (> 200 M) and higher daily average volume (> 10,000 shares).

VI   Research stocks by Technical Analysis

6   Do

When the stock, the sector that the stock is in and the market both are above its SMA-n averages (Single Moving Average for n days), it is a buy.

1. Bring up finviz.com from your browser.

2. Enter SPY. Write down the SMA-200 (Single Moving Average for 200 days). Positive numbers indicate the trend for the market is good.

   However, the market could be peaking or overbought. Do not buy stocks when SMA-200 is over 5% and / or RSI(14) is over 65%. RSI is a metric in the same screen.

3. Enter the sector ETF (check ETF in Chapter 14) the stock is in. Write down the SMA-50. Positive numbers indicate trend for the sector is good.

   However, the sector could be peaking or overbought. Do not buy stocks when SMA-200 is over 10% and / or RSI(14) is over 65%. RSI is a metric in the same screen.

4. Enter the stock symbol. If your average holding period of the stocks is 50, use SMA-50 and so on. I recommend SMA-200 for holding stocks long term. Write down the SMA-n for your stock. Positive numbers indicate the trend is good.

   However, the market could be peaking or overbought. Do not buy stocks when SMA-200 is over 25% and / or RSI(14) is over 70%. RSI is a metric in the same screen.

If the above three criteria and the fundamental criteria are satisfied, most likely it is a good buy.

Be aware that this discipline requires you spending a lot of time on the screen. That's the reason you do not want to keep more than 15 stocks for this style of investing.

I use technical analysis sparingly on stocks due to my lack of time but I usually marry it with fundamentals.

I use technical analysis more frequently to detect market crashes and sectors that proves to be a better indicator than stocks. Technical indicators usually work better in shorter durations.

My additions to conventional swing trading

Hopefully my additions improve the performance of a strategy that already works.

- I add market timing to Swing Trading. You need to sell most stocks during a market plunge (of course better selling at the peak) and buy them back when the chart indicates so.

- Diversify your portfolio. Keep less than 15 stocks for a portfolio less than a million. Ensure not more than 3 stocks in the same sector. Keep 20 stocks for portfolio over a million. Too many stocks would require more of your time that would be better spent in evaluating stocks. Too few stocks would impact your portfolio when one stock has a big loss.

- Stick with stocks over $2, average daily volume over 8,000 shares (or 6,000 shares for price over $20) and market cap over 200 million in the major three exchanges.

    Most big winners usually are in the price range between $2 and $12 price, and market cap between 200 million to 800 million. These stocks are ignored by the institution investors due to their restrictions. There are exceptions. Adjust the criteria according to your requirements.

- Ignore the subscription services claiming making more than 30% profit consistently. Some even have examples of making 5,000%. Most likely they tell you the winners but not their losers. When they back test their strategies, they cheat their performances with survivorship bias (i.e. those bankrupt stocks are not in the historical database). If their returns are that great, do you think they will share their secrets with you?

VII Bonus

7 The best strategy

This is the strategy I use every week when the market is not plunging or peaking.

Based on my investment with many subscription services (with a total cost of less than $1,000 per year), I do not have to use the free screening method described. When you have the size of my portfolio, it would be "pound stupid and penny smart" not to subscribe these investment services.

It would not be appropriate to recommend any subscription services here. When they are in business for over 5 years, most likely they are fine. However, they may not perform well recently due to their methods may not be suitable to the current market conditions.

Most offer a month free trial. Set up the screeners as described for all 3 strategies or just the one you will use most. Test out their performance as the durations described. Vary the parameters. Compare the returns to SPY, an ETF simulating the S&P 500 index.

If they have a historical database, a month should be enough. Without a historical database, you have to wait longer to calculate the performances and your test is limited. Hopefully you can test the screens in both a rising market and a falling market.

For this strategy, I use the timing grades. Most subscriptions provide several grades: composite grade, fundamental grade and timing grade (which could be termed as momentum grade).

Compare the grades from several subscription services. If all point out to be positive for a stock, most likely it will be fine. You may want to have a grade yourself composing all these timing grades from subscriptions.
Strategy #2.

This strategy is in the middle ground of the three strategies. It uses fundamentals more than strategy #1.

It is the strategy I use for sector rotation as my annuity provides sector funds that can be rotated every two months without penalty.

Strategy #3.

Among the 3, this strategy has higher chance to keep the stock for a year to qualify for the favorable treatment of long term capital gain.

After three months of holding, check whether it is still worth to hold. If so, hold it for another three months, and so on.

When it suffers a loss and the holding period is less than 365, sell it to qualify for short-term capital loss. If not, wait for one more day, sell covered call to generate some income. Check the current tax law on capital gains.

8   Tom's conservative strategy

The following is a summary of Tom's conservative strategy as described in his profile in Seeking Alpha web site. Use it as an example and modify it to fit your investing philosophy. You need to ignore your friends telling you how much money he is making when the market is up. You also need not to tell them how much money you're not losing otherwise you do not have any friend.

I believe the best performance is achieved matching a strategy to the current market conditions and there is no Holy Grail in investing.

Click here for Tom's strategy.
(http://tonyp4idea.blogspot.com/2012/05/tom-armisteads-investment-strategy.html)

A winning strategy for couch potatoes

My friend Tom (no relationship) has a very similar strategy similar to Tom's. My friend is making money with the least risk. He only buys stocks after the market crashes and sell stocks when the market rises. Ignore all market pundits. It is recommended to anyone who does not have time to monitor his/her investment.

Enhance a good strategy.
Following the favorable stages to trade in the market cycle described in this book, buy in the Early Recovery phase (about 1 ½ year after the crash or use the entry point described in the chapters on Market Timing), sell in one or two years after and maintain cash for the rest of the time.

Optionally add a small amount of purchases in Nov. 1 and sell them in April 1. Optionally buy in Dec. 1 and sell in Feb. 1 to take advantage of the best (statistically) period of the year. Add long term bonds when the interest rate is high (say more than 5%) and you do not have to sell these bonds.

Spend the rest of the time in the comfortable couch (i.e. enjoying life) or sip some fancy tropical drink served by some beautiful tropical lady in some nice tropical island. Not a bad strategy!

Top down approach

1. Is it a good time to buy stocks (via market timing)?
2. What sectors to buy?
3. Screen out about 10 stocks in that sector.
4. Further evaluate each stock.
5. Optionally, use Technical Analysis to see the best time and price to buy the selected stocks.
6. Periodically monitor your stocks. Sell some if necessary and go to Step 1.

When you buy at the bottom, buy value stocks only.

The easiest retirement planning system

Have a budget and live within your means. Buy good stuffs that last for a long time. After saving enough cash for emergency and planned expenses such as vacation, new car, college, etc., invest your extra money in a retirement account (Roth IRA if allowable) with 80% in a market ETF and 20% in a short-term bond ETF.

Run the chart described in the market cycle chapters once a month. If the chart tells you to exit the market, move all to cash. Reenter the market when the chart tells you so. It beats most if not all of your financial plans from the best experts money can buy.

Afterthoughts

My late friend had a 'buy and hold strategy' that worked pretty well. Most of his stocks were big companies. He died with a house worth more than a million and many millions in stocks. His only mistake was not to transfer more of his stocks to his heirs before his death. He died on the year when the estate exemption returned back to a million. Uncle Sam was the biggest winner and won big without any effort.

9 Trade plan

You should have a trade plan. It should include the following basics:

1. Objective.
2. When, what stocks and how many to buy.
3. When and what stocks to sell.
4. When and how to monitor your trading strategies.

The follow is my suggestion. Adjust them according to your personal requirements.

Be disciplined

It would make your trading to be a discipline which will provide better results in the long run and save you time. Following the trade plan would not allow your emotion to take over.

To illustrate, you have a specific day (Monday or the first day of the month) to check the value of your portfolio. Checking it several times a day is a waste of energy and it could cause harm to your emotions.

Objective

Set up your objective and requirements first. Your objective could be seeking the highest profit, profit at the least risk, protecting principle, generating income or a combination. Beating the market should not be your primary objective.

For example, a better objective is making more than 5% per year in the next 10 years at the least risk. Why 5%? I estimate we have 3% inflation and 2% taxes.

You can be conservative and aggressive at the same time by setting up two accounts, one for each objective. In addition, you may want to define the maximum investment amount for each account.

I have three objectives and they usually fall into different accounts and different holding periods.

- Profit at the least risk. Buy value stocks. Review bought stocks every 6 months. Non-taxable account.
- Momentum. Buy momentum stocks for maximum short-term (1 month) profits. Roth account.
- Conservative. Define a larger safety net. Conserve cash. Move all to stocks only when the market is most favorable.

Contrary to the above, most investors' or traders' objective is beating the market by a specific percent. It is fine too to measure how you perform against the market. For ultra conservative investors, not losing money is the primary objective.

If you made 10% and the market was up by 20%, you did not do good performance wise. However, do not blame yourself if your primary objective is conserving wealth. Most likely you had a high percent of your portfolio in cash and/or safer investments which do not appreciate a lot but they conserve your wealth.

Be flexible

Every one's trade plan is different. You should start a simple one and add features that would be useful to you. Keep it simple as you will not follow a complicated one.

Other features are: how you screen stocks, your average holding period, tax consequences, performance monitor, etc. This chapter shows you the very basics of a trade plan and you should start one if you do not have one.

You can refer to any chapter of this book in your trade plan. To illustrate, refer to the chapters when to sell a stock and spotting market plunges.

You can change your objective. When the market is risky, you want to be more conservative for example.

Disciplined but adaptive
Stick with the plan consistently. When your strategy that has been proven before does not work now, you should still stick to it. It is a common mistake for traders switching different technical indicator when the current one does not work. It explains why most beginner traders lose money.

It should be adaptive. When the current market favors growth, stick with a growth strategy.

A sample trade plan
You can review what stocks to buy and sell once a week or once a month depending on how active you are in the market. List the criteria you want to buy. Define your average holding period for a specific objective. Also define when and why you want to sell a stock.

Personally I prefer to have two sections: Common Tasks and Specific Tasks. Common Tasks includes 4 categories: Weekly Tasks, Monthly Tasks, Quarterly Tasks and Yearly Tasks. Evaluate stocks to buy on Tuesday every week for example. Update the portfolio and check out the chart on marketing timing on the first week of every month. Review performance of the portfolio quarterly (or half a year). Perform year-end tasks.

Specific Tasks include tasks I have to do on specific dates such as filing tax return, transferring stocks to my children and renewing investing subscriptions.

Weekly Tasks:

Mon	Covered calls
	IBD-50 review
Tue	Momentum strategy
Wed	Sell Momentum stocks over 2 weeks.

Monthly Tasks:

Mon	Performance monitor.
	Market timing: Market & Correction.
Tue	Find stocks using selected strategies.
	Find stocks using screens.
Wed	Evaluate stocks
Thur.	Buy stocks
	Sector rotation.
Fri	Evaluate any stocks to sell.
Any	Monitor momentum performance.

Quarterly Tasks:

1	Monthly tasks.
2	Performance monitor.

Year-end Tasks:

1	Tax adjustments for taxable

	accounts.
2	EOY purchases.
3	Spreadsheet for taxable accounts.
4	Fully invested in Dec. 15-Jan. 15
5	Screen performance monitor.
6	Dogs of DOW.

Review your performance and the trade plan

If you do not know what you did, how can you know what you're going? Review every trade transaction and monitor their performances.

Learn from your losses. Did you stick to the trade plan? If you lose too many times and/or take too much risk (evidenced by many losses and/or big losses), you may have to modify your trade plan. However, the trade plan may not be good to the current market (for example trading growth stocks in the bottom of the market cycle).

If you have to let the winners get away too often, review what's wrong. Sometimes, a lesson is not a lesson but just bad luck.

Learn about yourself
Learn about your risk tolerance, how mentally prepared are you on big losses and big wins. If you have more money than you can use for the rest of your life, conserving wealth should be your primary objective.

To illustrate with a portfolio of one million, your average stock position is $100,000 if you only have time to follow 10 stocks.

To many, the portfolio with 10 stocks is quite risky. You may consider having 10 stocks of $50,000 each and invest the rest ($500,000) in ETFs, mutual funds and/or bonds. Ensure no three or more stocks (some prefer 2) are in the same sector.

Prepare for some losses. Reduce the average loss to small amounts. I prefer 25% maximum loss for volatile stocks and 20% for other stocks. Some prefer using stop loss orders of 10% to 15% loss. Today's market is too volatile to stop losses less than 15%. One's opinion. You should have some big winners but let them getting away by selling them too early. One way is to use stop orders (10% less than the market price) and adjust the stops periodically (say a month) for the appreciating stocks.

A Quickie
Write down your objective and what tasks you do every week, month and year in the inside back cover in this book (hard copy only). If you do not do it now, you will never do it.

Trade journal
Keep a journal of your trades and ideas. Review it from time to time why you bought a specific stock. It is far better than recalling the experiences from memory.

Everyone should have a book such as this one to record their experiences. I do not recommend publishing one. You should spend your time in investing. Unless you're famous, most likely publishing is not profitable.

It should be part of a trade plan. You use it to monitor your performance of your trade. When you use a screen that is for short term, you want to exit the trade accordingly. When the screen does not perform, it may mean the market is not favorable to this screen and you should skip using it with actual money.

10   A turnaround strategy for value stocks

Many value stocks tend to stay in this phase for a long time. When the turnaround starts, it could be very profitable.

Market Timing

Do not buy any stock when the market is risky as described elsewhere in the book. Actually you should sell most of the stocks when the market is risky.

Buy Metrics

Metric	Value	Conservative	Aggressive
General			
Market Cap	>300 M	>1,000 M	>100 M
Price	> 2	>10	>1
Avg. Volume	>20,000	>50,000	>10,000

USA	Only	Only	Foreign but listed in USA
Fundamental			
Forward P/E	<15	<10	<25
Earning Gr Q-Q	>5%	>8%	>3%
ROE	>10	>15	>5
P / FCF	<10	<8	<15
Debt / Equity	<.5	<.25	<1
Technical			
SMA-50%	>10	>15	>5
Misc.			
Blue Chip Growth	A or B	A	A or B
Fidelity	>6	>8	>5
IBD	>60	>90	>50
Vector Vest	>=1	>=0.8	>=12
Value Line Proj. 3-5% return	>5%	>10%	>5%
Zacks	>=4	5	>=4
ASSS	>=2	>=5	>=2

The assignment values for the metrics are not fixed; feel free to change it according to your own risk level. I do have suggestions for conservative investors and aggressive investors.

Some of the metrics are not readily available in Finviz.com and the following describes how to modify them.

Explanation

- Market Cap. The free version of Finviz.com does not allow you to specify the range. Use 'Any' and then select the stocks according to the specified values. Average Volume has the similar restriction.
- The conservative values for Market Cap, Price and Average Volume try to select larger companies. The aggressive values try to select smaller companies, which historically are more risky but perform better.

- I prefer 'USA' for Country. Stay away from small companies from developing countries unless you can trust their financial statements.
- Forward P/E measures the value of the stock. Ensure "E" (Earnings) is positive. I prefer it over P/E (from the last twelve months).
- Earnings Growth Quarter to last Quarter is preferred to be positive unless it is during a recession.
- ROE measures how well the company has been managed.
- P/FCF. "Price / Free Cash Flow" cannot be manipulated easily. Together with low "Debt / Equity", it measures whether the company would bankrupt.
- SMA-50%. Some stocks tend to stay in a value stage for a long while (termed value trap). We like to select stocks just starting being noticed and on its way up.
- Misc. Many sites have evaluated the stocks for us. Some only let their customers to access such information, some are available for free trials or are available from the library.
- ASSS is my scoring system.

With the above, I have 35 stocks on 10/28/16. If you need 10 stocks for further evaluation, try to sort Forward P/E in descending order and select the top 10. If you cannot find any or substantially less than normal, it implies the market is risky, so take a break. If the performances of the last few stocks you selected are poor, take a break too as the market conditions do not favor the value metrics we specified.

Qualitative analysis
Double click on the stock and read as many articles described on the stock as possible. If it meets all the criteria, buy the stock. Recommend to use market orders for large companies in a non-volatile market (when the average daily fluctuation is less than 0.5%). If the selected stock is the one you just sold, make you only buy it after 31 days to avoid Wash Sale penalty.

Keeping informed

Check the company updates of the stock you owned every month. One easy way is to enter the stocks in a portfolio in SeekingAlpha.com.

Sell the stock

Re-evaluate the stocks every 6 months.

If it does not meet the criteria or the market is risky, sell it. If it is only a few days away from the long-term capital gain, sell the losers right away or hold on the winner for a few more days.

Re-balance the portfolio after a stock has been sold. Ensure it is diversified enough into large/small cap and sectors.

Top-down Investing

It is similar to the above. Find the sectors that perform the best last month. Under Finviz.com, select the best sector under 'sector' one at a time. Several sites such as Fidelity compare the stock to the averages of stocks in the same sector.

Appendix 1 – All my books

The Kindle version of Complete the Art of Investing: 16 books in one, over 900 pages (6*9) or about the size of 3 average books on investing and highly recommended. My other investing books can be grouped as follows.

- The following books are in a series: Finding Profitable Stocks, Market Timing and Scoring Stocks (or Modern Security Analysis: Simple & Effective).

- Books for today's market: Profit from 2017 Market Crash and Best Stocks (check any current offer).

- Books on strategies: Swing (Rotation + Momentum), Sector Rotation, ETF Rotation for Couch Potatoes, Momentum, SuperStocks, Dividend, Penny & Micro Stock, and Retiree. If you are into Rotation and Momentum, order Swing as it has several new chapters not found in "Complete The Art of Investing".

- Books for advance beginners: billionaire (perfect gift for recent college graduates and they will thank you when they become

- billionaires), Investing for Beginners, Profit via ETFs, Buffett, Ideas, Conservative and Top-Down.

- Miscellaneous. Lessons in Investing. Investing Strategies. Global Economies. Buy Low and Sell High. Buy High and sell Higher. Buffettology. Technical Analysis. Trading Stocks. A Nation of No Losers. Can China Say No. Several books on travel.

- Concise Editions and Introduction Editions are available at very low prices and are competitive to books of similar sizes (50 pages) and prices ($3 range).

For paperback & Nook. Search my books with "Tony Pow". Amazon's Match feature gives you a Kindle copy free (for most of my books) when you order the paperback. So, you have two books for the price of one.
My blog (www.TonyP4Idea.blogspot.com).
Links are subject to changes without notices.

Appendix 2 – Complete Art of Investing

Instead of buying 16 books, why not buy one book (Complete The Art of Investing) consisting of 16 books? Besides saving money and your digital shelve space, it gives you quick reference and concentration on the topic you're currently interested in. It covers most investing topics in investing excluding speculative investing such as currency trading and day trading.

The Kindle version has over 890 pages (6*9), about the size of three books of average size. With the cost of $10 and at least 1,000 investing ideas, it is less than one cent per idea. Most books have only a few ideas in the entire book.

The 16 books

This book "Complete Art of Investing" is divided into 16 books as follows. Click for the link to the book described in Amazon.com. I squeezed more than 3,000 pages into 890 pages by eliminating duplicated information such as evaluating stocks.

Book No.	Amazon.com
1	Beginner & Billionaire
2	Finding Stocks
3	Evaluating Stocks
4	Scoring Stocks
5	Trading Stocks
6	Market Timing
7	Strategies
8	Sector Rotation
9	Insider Trading
10	Penny Stocks & Micro Cap
11	Momentum Investing
12	Dividend Investing
13	Technical Analysis
14	Investing Ideas
15	The Economy
16	Buffettology

The book links are subject to change without notice.

"How to be a billionaire" is for beginners and couch potatoes, who can use the advanced features of this book in the simplest and less time-consuming techniques. Most advance users can skip this section unless they want to use some of the short cuts described.

We start with the basic books Finding Stocks, Evaluate Stocks, Trading Stocks and Market Timing. You can select and start with one of the many styles and strategies in investing such as swing trading and top-down strategy. Many tools are described in other books such as ETFs, technical analysis, covered calls and trade plan.

Many books start with "Why" to lure you to read more and are followed by "How" and then the theory behind the book.

Many books have common chapters such as Market Timing, Finding Stocks and Scoring Stocks. That's the reason I can squeeze over 2,000 pages into this book. Currently the printed version is not available due to the expensive paper cost for this lengthy book.

If the book you're reading is beneficial to you, imagine how it would with 900 pages.

#
The following are from readers of this book, "Debunk the Myths in Investing" or "The Art of Investing", which this book is derived from. As of 9/2016, I do not know the reviewers.

"Debunk the Myths in Investing is an all-encompassing look at not only the most salient factors influencing markets and investors, but also a from-the-trenches look at many of the misconceptions and mistakes too many investors make. Reading this book may save not only time and aggravation but money as well!"

By Joseph Shaefer, CEO, Stanford Wealth Management LLC. 11/2013.

"'Debunk the Myths in Investing' is an interesting book that on its 500 pages offer a lot of knowledge related to investing world and many practical advices, so I can recommend its reading if you're interested in this topic."

By Denis Vukosav, TOP 1000 REVIEWER 3/2014.

"490 pages of a genius's ranting and hypothesis with various theories throughout, written light-heartedly with ample doses of humor... Excellent market timing strategies. Yes, the myth of not being able to profitably time the market is BUSTED..." By Abe Vigoda 7/2014

"I just bought this book due to the woes of opening market 2016 and being brand new to investing, my eyes were crossed with all the different reasons we were/ are and what one can do to "manipulate the market". Investment Advices just to his research is phenomenal and doesn't overwhelm with big words or catchy "sales-like" tactics.

I truly believe this ordinary man, Mr. Tony Pow, has a gift of explaining his experience as an investor without the bull crap of trying to make you buy his stuff. He seemingly just wants to share his knowledge, tips, and clarity of definitions for the kind of folks like me who want to understand something FIRST before jumping in with emotions of trying to make a boat load of money. I like the technical analysis side he brings.

Mr. Tony Pow talks about hidden gems in his book, well....quite frankly, he is a hidden gem. Thank you and I will also post my comments about this author to my Facebook page!" – JB on this book 1/2016.
– JB on this book, Jan. 2016.

"Excellent book, recommend to all investors... great knowledge. It has fine-tuned my investing strategies... Your book is hard to set aside, as I read it all the time learning good techniques and analysis of stocks, ETF... Since I purchased your book in March, I have underlined, highlighted and placed tabs on top of pages for quick reference." – Aileron on this book, July, 2016.

I challenged to have the best-performed article in Seeking Alpha history, an investing site, for recommending 5 or more stocks in one year after the publish date. The concepts for that article are discussed in this book.
http://seekingalpha.com/article/2492255-a-tale-of-2-portfolios

Appendix 3 - Our window to the investing world

This is a summary of the web sites described in this book and the web sites you may want to refer to. Click on the sites and a brief comment may be included. The paperback version of this chapter can be found in the following link.

http://ebmyth.blogspot.com/2013/11/web-sites.html

- **General**
  Wikipedia / Investopedia / Yahoo!Finance / MarketWatch / Cnnfn / Morningstar /

  CNBC / Bloomberg / WSJ / Barron's / Motley Fool / TheStreet

  Understanding the news is fine but most likely you will not profit directly from the news. Read the chapter on Headlines to interpret the news and profit from it.

- **Evaluate stocks**
  Finviz / SeekingAlpha / MSN Money / Zacks / Daily Finance / ADR / Fidelity / BlueChipGrowth / Earnings Impact / OpenInsider / NYSE / NASDAQ / SEC /

  SEC for 10K and 10Q (quarterly) reports required to file for listed stocks in major exchanges.

- **Charts**
  BigCharts / FreeStockCharts / StockCharts /

- **Screens**
  Yahoo!Finance / Finviz / CNBC / Morningstar /

- **Besides stocks**
  123Jump / Hoover's Online / FINRA Bond Market Data / REIT / Commodity Futures /

  Option Industry

- **Vendors**
  AAII / Zacks / IBD / GuruFocus / Vector Vest /

  Fidelity / Interactive Brokers / Merrill Lynch /

Fidelity has extensive research and I feel they have excellent executions in trades. Interactive Brokers is least expensive to trade options and their interest rates are low. Merrill Lynch provides 30-commission free trades per month for a deposit requirement in the bank; check their current offer.

- **Economy.**
  Econday / EcoconStats / Federal Reserve / Economist /

- **Misc.**
  Dow Jones Indices / Russell / Wilshire /

  IRS / Wikinvest /

  ETF Database / ETF Trends /

  Nolo (estate planning) / AARP /

Appendix 4 - ETFs / Mutual Funds

What is an ETF

Fidelity: Index ETFs (https://www.fidelity.com/etfs/overview).

Wikipedia on ETF (http://en.wikipedia.org/wiki/Exchange-traded_fund).

List of ETFs

ETF Bloomberg
http://www.bloomberg.com/markets/etfs/
ETF data base
http://etfdb.com/
ETF Trends
http://www.etftrends.com/
A list of ETFs. Seeking Alpha.
(http://etf.stock-encyclopedia.com/category/)

Fidelity's commission-free ETFs.
(https://www.fidelity.com/etfs/ishares)

Fidelity Annuity funds with performance data.
http://fundresearch.fidelity.com/annuities/category-performance-annual-total-returns-quarterly/FPRAI?refann=005

A list of contra ETFs (or bear ETFs)
http://www.tradermike.net/inverse-short-etfs-bearish-etf-funds/

Misc.: Seeking Alpha, ETFGuide, ETFReplay (highly recommended for the historical database).

Other resources

Your broker should have a lot of information on ETFs and many offer commission-free ETFs.

Most subscription services offer research on ETFs. IBD has a strategy dedicated to ETFs and so is AAII to name a couple.

Seeking Alpha has extensive resources for ETF including an ETF screener and investing ideas.

Not all ETFs are created equal

Check their performances and their expenses. If there are two similar ETFs, check out the expense ratio. For example, I prefer IVV over SPY for lower fee (.04% vs. .0945% as of 4/2017). Fidelity offers commission-free ETFs. Check out their current and your broker's offerings.
(https://www.fidelity.com/etfs/ishares)

Most of the time some ETFs are correlated such as Gold and Gold Miner. If they are not, their performances would likely merge. Hence, you may want to buy the one that has worse performance and expect it to rise back to the same level as the other one.

Investing into two ETFs that have the same objective such as SPY and IVV does not make sense.

SPY simulating S&P 500 is weighted by market cap. If not, all the 500 stocks should weigh .2% as 500 * .2% = 100%. As of 6/1/2017, it has 4% on APPL, 3% on MSFT, 2% on AMZN and FB. All these four stocks are rocket stocks. I bet when they fall, they would fall faster. Hence it affects the performance of SPY.

Small but well-performed ETFs

Here is a list.
http://finance.yahoo.com/news/small-etfs-pack-big-punch-195430875.html

Guggenheim Spin-Off ETF (CSD) looks interesting. The ETF tracks corporate spinoffs. It has beaten SPY for a long while; check the current performance. Not a recommendation.

When not to use ETFs
I prefer sector mutual funds in some industries that need to extensive research. They are drug industry, banks, miners and insurers. Most ETFs cannot exclude stocks from a specific sector such as risky Chinese banks from FXI.

Half ETF
Taking out half of the stocks that score below the average in an index ETF could beat the same full ETF itself. I call it HETF (half the ETF). You hear it here first. I hope all the fund creators of HETF (trademark pending ☺) will donate to my secret retiring fund for using the name and my concept.

To illustrate, sort the expected P/E (not including stocks with negative earnings) in ascending order and only include the stocks on the first half. Add more fundamental metrics. It will take minutes.

Disadvantages of ETFs

- When you have two stocks in a sector ETF one good one and one bad one, the ETF treats them the same. Stock pickers would buy the one with better appreciation potential.
- The return is better than the actual return due to stock rotation. To illustrate, on August 29, 2012, SHLD was replaced by LYB in a sector fund. SHLD was down by 4% and LYB was up by 4% primarily due to the switch. Unless you sell and buy at the right time (that's impossible), your return would not match with the ETF's return due to the replacement.

- Ensure the performance matches the corresponding index, which is most likely does not include dividends.

Advantages of ETFs

- We have demonstrated you can beat the market by using market timing. Between 2000 and Nov., 2013, you only exit and reenter the market 3 times and the result is astonishing.
- It is easy to rotate a sector vs. buying/selling all stocks in this sector. It makes sector rotation the same as trading a stock.
- The risk is spread out and your portfolio is diversified especially for a market ETF or buying three or more ETFs in different sectors.
- Eliminate the time in researching stocks.

Leveraged ETFs

I do not recommend them. Some are 2x, 3x and even higher. They're too risky. However, when you are very sure or your strategy has very low drawdown, you may want to use them to improve performance. I recommend skipping all leveraged ETFs.

My basic ETF tables

I use a list of selected ETFs and commission-free (check details) ETFs from Fidelity for my purpose. I include some mutual funds and mutual funds for Fidelity's annuity. Some may be interesting to you. I use ETFs for sector rotation and parking my cash when the market is favorable and I do not have stocks I want to buy.

ETFs and funds come and go. Some ideas and classifications are my interpretation.

Table by market cap:

Category	ETF	Fidelity ETF	Mutual Funds	Fidelity's Annuity	Contra ETF
Size:					
Large Cap	DIA		See Blend		DOG
	SPY				SH
	QQQ	ONEQ			PSQ
	RYH				
Blend	IWD	IVV	BEQGX		
Growth	SPYG	IVW	FBGRX		
Value	SPYV		DOGGX		
Dividend	NOBL	DVY	FRDPX		
	VYM				
Mid Cap				FNBSC	MYY
Blend	MDY	JJH	VSEQX		
Growth		IJK	STDIX		
			BPTRX		
Value		IJJ	FSMVX		
Small Cap				FPRGC	SBB
Blend	IWM	IJR	HDPSX		
Growth		IJT	PRDSX		
Value		IJS	SKSEX		
Micro	IWC				
Multi					
Blend			VDEOX		
Growth			VHCOX		
Value			TCLCX		
Bond					
Long-term Treasury	TLT				TBF
Long Term (20)	VLV		BTTTX		
Mid Term (7 – 10)	VCIT		FSTGX		
Short Term (1 – 3 yrs.)	VCSH		THOPX		
Total	BOND		PONDX		
Corp Invest Grade			NTHEX		
High Yield (junk)	PHB		SPHIX		
Muni	MUB		Check state		

Special situation				
Buy back	PKW			
Momentum	MTUM			

Table by sectors:

Sector	ETF	Fidelity ETF	Mutual Funds	Fidelity's Annuity
Bank[1]	KBE			
Bio	IBB		FBIOX	
	XBI		Large	
Consumer Dis.	XLY	FDIS	FSCPX	FVHAC
Consumer Staple	XLP	FSTA	FDFAX	FCSAC
Finance	KIE	FNCL	FIDSX	FONNC
	IYF			
Energy	XLE	FENY	FSENX	FJLLC
Energy Service			FSESX	
Gold	GLD		FSAGX	
Gold Miner	GDX		VGPMX	
Health Care	IYH	FHLC	FSPHX	FPDRC
	VHT		VGHCX	
House Builder	ITB		FSHOX	
			Perform	
Industrial	IYJ	FIDU	FCYIX	FBALC
Material	VAW	FMAT	FSDPX	
	IYM			
	XME			
Oil	USO			
Oil Service	OIH		FSESX	
Oil Exploration	XOP			
Gas	UNG			
Real Estate	VNQ		FRIFX	FFWLC
Retail	RTH		FSRPX	
	XRT			
Regional bank	KRE		FSRBX	
Semi Conduct	SMH			
Software	XSW		FSCSX	
	IGV			
Technology	XLK	FTEC	FSPTX	FYENC
	FDN		FBSOX	

			ROGSX	
Telecomm.	VOX	FCOM	FSTCX	FVTAC
Transport	XTN			
	IYT			
Utilities	XLU	FUTY	FSUTX	FKMSC
Wireless			FWRLX	

Footnote. [1] Also check Finance.

Table by countries:

Country	ETF	Fidelity ETF	Mutual Funds	Fidelity's Annuity
Australia	EWA			
Brazil	EWZ			
Canada	EWC		FICDX	
China	FXI		FHKCX	
Greece	GREK			
India	INDY		MINDX	
Indonesia	EIDO			
Nordic			FNORX	
Hong Kong	EWH			
Japan	EWJ		FJPNX	
S. Africa	EZA			
S. Korea			MAKOX	
Singapore	EWS			
Taiwan	EWT			
Turkey	TUR			
United Kingdom	EWU			
Vietnam	VNM			
Combination	1	2	3	4
Intern. Div.	IDV	DWX		
Small Cap	SCZ	GWX		
Value	EFV			
EAFE	EFA			
Emerging	VWO		FEMEX	FEMAC
Europe	VGK		FIEUX	
Global	KXI		PGVFX	
Latin America	ILF		FLATX	

Quick analysis of ETFs

Evaluate an ETF

ETF is a basket of stocks according to a specific sector, country or a theme.

Yahoo!Finance used to give the P/E of an ETF. Try to get it from ETFdb.com. If it is below 15 and above zero, it could be a value ETF. Also, if the current price is lower than its NAV, it is sold with discount (or premium vice versa). Compare its YTD Return to SPY's.

From Finviz.com, enter the ETF symbol. If SMA-20%, SMA-50% and SMA-200% are all positive, most likely the ETF is in uptrend. To illustrate, SMA-200 is Simple Moving Average for the last 200 trade sessions (no trading on weekends and specific holidays). The percent is how much the stock price of the ETF above the SMA. If the percent is negative, it means the stock price is below the SMA.

If your average holding period is about 50 days, SMA-50% is more appropriate to you for example.

If RSI(14) > 70, it is probably over-sold; if it is < 35, it is probably under-sold (i.e. value).

In addition, ensure the average volume is high (more than 10,000 shares to me), market cap is more than 200 M, and it has low fee. Most popular ETFs have these characteristics. Avoid leveraged ETFs for now.

How to determine the sector has been recovered
It is easier to profit by following the uptrend of an ETF using the above info. It is hard to detect when the bottom of an ETF has been reached. If SMA-20%, SMA-50% and SMA-200% are all positive, most likely the ETF is in uptrend or it has recovered. It does not always happen as predicted, so use stops to protect your investment.

An example
This example illustrates how to evaluate ETFs. First, determine whether the market is risky. Most beginners should not invest in a risky market. Advance investors can bet against the market or a specific sector by buying contra ETFs or puts.

Next, you want to limit the number of sector ETFs by selecting those that are either trending up or hitting bottom (bottom is harder to predict). Personally I prefer sectors with long-term uptrend (indicated by cnnfn.com). Seeking Alpha has many current articles on ETFs.

Today's market (as of 2/5/2016) is risky. For illustration only, I select the following ETFs: SPY (simulating the market based on large companies), XLP (consumer staples) and XLY (consumer discretionary). XLP should perform better than XLY during a recession as those products are the necessities.

Technical indicators such as SMA-50 (Simple Moving Average for the last 50 sessions), SMA-200 and RSI(14) are from finviz.com and the rest are from Yahoo!Finance.com. After you buy the ETF, use stop loss to protect your investment. Bio tech sector moved up for many months until it crashed later in 2015.

As of 2/5/2016	SPY	XLP (staples)	XLY (discret.)
Price	190	50	71
NAV	192	50	73
• Technical			
SMA-50	-4%	0%	-7%
SMA-200	-6%	2%	-7%
RSI(14)	44	50	36
Other	Double bottom at $186		
• Fundamental			
P/E	17	20	19
Yield	2.1%	2.5%	1.5%
YTD return	-5%	0.5%	-5%
Net asset	174 B	9 B	10 B

Explanation
- The figures may not be identical from the two web sites due to the dates they use.
- XLY has better discount among the 3 ETFs as most investors believe a recession is coming.
- XLP has less down trend among the 3 ETFs as expected.
- XLY is more undersold among the 3 as expected.
- Double bottom is a technical pattern that indicates the stock would surge.
- SPY has better valued according to its P/E.

- XLY's dividend is the least among the 3 as they have more tech companies in the ETF. They have to plow back the profits to research and development.
- XLP has the best YTD return among the 3.
- As long as the asset is above 500 M (200 M for specialized ETFs), it is fine and all three pass this mark.

There are many metrics such as Debt/Equity not available from these two web sites. Many sites list the top holding of a specific ETF. Just average the metrics of the top ten or so of its stock holdings.

Rotation of 4 ETFs

We can beat the market by rotating one ETF that represents the market such as SPY and cash (or short-term bond ETF) via market timing.

During market uptrend, rotate the following four ETFs could be more profitable. Be warned that short-term capital gain in taxable accounts is not treated as favorably as the long-term capital gain; check current tax laws.

The allocation percentages depend on individual risk tolerance. You can use indexed mutual funds. Compare their expenses and restrictions. Some mutual funds charge you if you withdraw within a specific period.

Select the best performer of last month (from Seeking Alpha, cnnFn, or the ETF/mutual fund site). I prefer 45 days instead of one month as they are not too volatile. Add sector ETFs to the four ETFs such as XLY, XLP, XLE, XLF, XLU, IYW, XHB, IYM, OIL and XLU to expand your selection.

ETFs	Money Market	US	International	Bond
Fidelity		Spartan Total Market	Spartan Global Market	Spartan US Bond
Vanguard		Total Stock Market	Total International Market	Total Bond Market
My choice	Fidelity	SPY	Vanguard	Fidelity
Suggest %				

During Market plunge	90%	0%	0%	10%
After plunge	10%	60%	10%	20%

Explanation
- The above are suggestions only. If your broker offers similar ETFs, consider using them.
- Check out any restrictions of the ETFs.
- 4 ETFs (one actually is a money market fund) are enough for most starters. They are diversified, low-cost and you do not need balancing except during market plunge (refer the chapter on Detecting Market Plunges).
- The percentages are suggestion only. If you are less risk tolerance, allocate more on money market fund and/or bond ETF.
- Have at least 10% allocated to the money market fund. When there is a mild market dip, move the money market fund to the US equity fund. Move it back to money market when there is a mild market upsurge. If you do not have time to check the market, allocate this 10% to the bond ETF.
- When the market is risky, reduce stock equities (i.e. increase money market and bond allocations).
- The symbols for Fidelity ETFs are FSTMX, FSGDX and FBIDX.
- The symbols for Vanguard ETFs are VTSMX, VGTSX and VBMFX.
- To boost performance, add GLD, the gold ETF.
- Again, do not invest during market plunge as indicated by my market timing techniques.

If you are more advanced, use additional sector ETFs to rotate. Find out the current winners from many sources including CNNfn.com. Also buy long-term bond funds (such as 30-year Treasury) when the interest rate is 10% or more. I have covered the basics in sector rotation.

Epilogue
Thanks for reading. If you find this book useful, please write a brief, unbiased review. When you have mastered the techniques in this book, read Appendix 2 for my book Complete the Art of Investing and the Kindle version has over 900 pages (6*9), about 3 times the average book on investing. As of 5/2017, I do not know any of my reviewers and all profits have been donated to charities.

Made in the USA
Columbia, SC
17 September 2018